THE HAMSTER
OPERA COMPANY

THE HAMSTER OPERA COMPANY

JANIS MITCHELL

Commentaries by Stanley Baron

With 31 color plates

THAMES AND HUDSON

Frontispiece
A rehearsal of *Tosca* with Lina Carpaccia in one of her most characteristic roles. In attendance are Ugo Rondetto (foreground left) and Filbert Broadstreet (foreground right). Between them is the somewhat bewildered director Harvey Icepick, who does not always see eye to eye with Carpaccia.

© 1988 Thames and Hudson Ltd, London

First published in the United States in 1988 by Thames and Hudson Inc., 500 Fifth Avenue, New York, New York 10110

Library of Congress Catalog Card Number 87–51152

Printed and bound in Hong Kong

The well-known millionaire philanthropist from Philadelphia, Filbert Broadstreet, was convinced by the history of the Hamster Ballet Company that an opera company along the same lines could enjoy a similar success. He was fortunate in securing as his impresario the fiery, dedicated Ugo Rondetto, who gathered under his wing a company of such quality that virtually every performance of the first season was sold out. Rondetto's greatest catch was that remarkable soprano Lina Carpaccia, whose dramatic presence and vocal accomplishments make her a star of stars. Here she is seen running through the famous aria 'Sempre libera' (Always Free), from *La Traviata*.

PAGLIACCI

Like most grand opera companies, the HOC finds the *Pag* and *Cav* double-bill a safe money-spinner. And with a star like Gino Peruzzi singing the part of Canio it becomes a memorable experience.

In Act II, the play within the play. Nedda is an anxious Columbine, her husband Canio is Pagliacci, and Beppe is Harlequin in the background. Canio is working himself into a jealous frenzy before stabbing his faithless wife to death in front of the audience.

CAVALLERIA RUSTICANA

This one-act opera of Sicilian passion and revenge is given a dynamic, compelling production by the HOC, with a colourful set and costumes by Jennifer Primrose. Here is the scene, after the villagers have come out of the church, when young Turiddu invites them to drink a glass in his mother's wineshop, and his rival Alfio scornfully refuses his offer of wine. This leads directly to the duel in which Turiddu is killed.

THE BARBER OF SEVILLE

Agile singers are required to match the verve of this Rossini comic opera, and Ugo Rondetto proved his skill as manager by introducing two real discoveries when it was first produced in this hamster version. For the part of Rosina, he found the sparkling soprano Dora Llandu singing in a Welsh chapel choir. His Figaro, Carlo Gigifazzi, was a budding dental technician in a small south Italian village.

In Act I Figaro sings the famous rapid aria in which he enumerates the various activities he undertakes as 'general factotum' to the city of Seville.

In the same Act, Rosina, though she is under the watchful eye of the pedantic music-master Basilio, manages to drop a note from the balcony intended for her unknown admirer, Count Almaviva, who began the Act by serenading her with a group of musicians.

At the end of the opera, in spite of a series of hilarious disguises and misunderstandings, the Count and his Rosina are united in marriage.

CARMEN

No opera company can afford to neglect Bizet's ever-popular masterpiece. In its very first season the HOC produced a robust and impassioned version of *Carmen* which was immediately hailed by critics and audiences alike. Billed as 'Carmen without frills', it features the mezzo-soprano Clara La Jolla as the wilful, fickle Gypsy girl whose actions lead to tragedy and death.

In Act II, set in the tavern of Lillas Pastia, she uses her wiles to persuade the infatuated corporal, Don José, to desert the army and join the band of smugglers with whom she has decided to go into the mountains. He does not resist her for long.

CARMEN

By the beginning of Act IV, Carmen has transferred her affections from the hapless Don José to the bullfighter Escamillo.

A crowd has gathered outside the arena of Seville where the popular Escamillo is to perform that day, and when he appears with Carmen on his arm they boisterously sing his praise. Escamillo and the crowd go into the arena, and Carmen is left alone to face Don José, who has come there in hopes of reviving her love for him. When she contemptuously rejects him, the ruined man kills her with a knife.

This exciting opera, supercharged with emotion and haunting rhythms, ends in a kind of stunned silence.

LA TRAVIATA

The role of Violetta in Verdi's adaptation of the Dumas play, *La Dame aux Camélias*, is one of Lina Carpaccia's favourites. Playing a party girl with a heart of gold and a serious case of tuberculosis, she has ideal opportunities to shine as the supreme actress-singer that she is.

In Act I a party is in full swing in Violetta's Paris house. Guests are merrily drinking champagne and dancing. But Alfredo, brought to the party by his friend Gaston, has fallen in love with their hostess and in this scene declares that love. As Alfredo, Gino Peruzzi is extremely effective in portraying the ardour of youth.

Carpaccia is such an accomplished performer that she manages, even in this first Act, to convey not only the delicacy of her love for Alfredo, but also the sacrifice she will make for him and his family before dying in his arms.

RIGOLETTO

The rich baritone role of Rigoletto in Verdi's perennially popular melodrama is taken by the veteran Herbert Jefferson, and he clearly relishes the character of the bitter hunchback jester who is indirectly responsible for the death of his own beloved daughter Gilda. Although Rigoletto has kept Gilda in seclusion, his master, the wicked Duke of Mantua, has ingratiated himself with her by pretending to be a student. Several of the Duke's courtiers, well pleased to avenge themselves on Rigoletto for insolent remarks he has made to them in the past, manage to kidnap Gilda with her father's unwitting help.

In Act II, Rigoletto finds his daughter in the Duke's palace. The disconsolate girl now knows that the Duke has duped her, and she and her father sing a sad duet.

Then Rigoletto sees another courtier being led to prison for betraying the Duke, and he sings the famous *aria di vendetta* in which he swears to avenge the wrong done to his daughter.

The coloratura part of Gilda is acted and sung with great confidence by Mercy Cristale, one of the rare French hamsters in the company.

MADAM BUTTERFLY

Ah, Madam Butterfly! Who can resist the bittersweet tale of a refined Japanese girl's love for a callous American naval officer in the early years of the twentieth century? No one can – at least when Gabriella Concile brings her dramatic soprano voice to the role. She manages to suggest Butterfly's vulnerable innocence to perfection.

In this scene in Act I, Butterfly and her family and friends arrive at the charming house where she and Lt. Pinkerton will be married and live together. Pinkerton, one of Caruso's famous roles, is usually sung in the HOC production by Gino Peruzzi.

MADAM BUTTERFLY

In Act III, three years after Pinkerton deserted Butterfly, he returns with his American wife, and Butterfly finally understands her betrayal. She prepares to give up her son 'Trouble' to his father before committing hara-kiri. Suzuki, her faithful servant, watches apprehensively from behind a screen.

The setting, with its screen of Fujiyama and the rising sun, has been much praised.

THE RING OF THE NIBELUNGS:
The Rhinegold

Rondetto's natural inclination is towards Italian, not German opera, but he is astute enough to recognize that an international company, such as Mr. Broadstreet envisaged, would have to give due weight to the German repertoire. He hired Gunther Winterstrebel to assist him in this area, and these two together created a Ring cycle which ranks among their most admirable undertakings.

The illustration shows the big moment towards the end of *The Rhinegold* (the Prologue to the three-part opera) when the gods are conducted by their leader Wotan to the castle of Valhalla. By this time the fateful gold has changed hands about three times and the Nibelungs' curse has begun to run its course.

THE VALKYRIES

For those who are not fond of Wagner's operas (and there are a fair number of them), the sight and sound of Brünnhilde singing her outburst of triumphant joy – *Ho yo to ho!* – are often the final straw. Most of the memorable Brünnhildes have been ample women, difficult to accept as young female warriors, which is what the Valkyries were.

The hamster Brünnhilde, Tilly Thunderbar, is certainly ample, but like that great Norwegian soprano Kirsten Flagstad she possesses a resonant, full voice with which she manages to convince her enthusiastic admirers that Wagner's epic of revenge, magic, love and destiny can actually be understood and enjoyed.

SIEGFRIED

In the second opera of the cycle, the true hero emerges. It is Siegfried who is pre-ordained to recover the gold for the gods. The first stage in this conquest takes place in Act II when Siegfried kills the giant Fafner, who has transformed himself into a ferocious dragon.

The HOC has called on the services of various tenors for their Siegfried; the most satisfactory and convincing has been Rex Tremolo, who seems to have the right voice and bearing for a hero with the heavy weight of destiny hanging over him.

BORIS GODOUNOV

It is indicative of Rondetto's breadth of vision that he should consider mounting this most difficult Russian opera, which demands a bass singer of the highest quality, as well as an enormous cast, an important chorus and a large number of scene changes. The HOC *Boris* has turned out to be a stunning spectacle with massive sets designed by Mary Ellen Turreen. The orchestra has proved to be equal to Moussorgsky's convoluted and expressive score.

But best of all is Derek Carthage, the hamster equivalent of the great Chaliapin who made the role famous in the early days of this century. Carthage's imposing appearance and his dark, deep voice have earned him public approval. He has also been impressive as Wotan in the Wagner *Ring*.

LA BOHEME

Ever since its premiere in 1896, Puccini's opera of life among the students and artists of Left Bank Paris has been a perennial favourite. Mercy Cristale has just the right kind of voice for the fragile character of Mimi. In the part of the poet Rodolfo, Ferruccio Nutti reminds old-timers of that wonderful star of the 1930s, Beniamino Gigli.

In Act I Mimi and Rodolfo have their chance meeting outside his attic room. In Act II the action shifts to the bustling streets on Christmas Eve, and particularly to the Café Momus, where a group of Rodolfo's boon companions are gathered. Here Musetta appears and sings her famous waltz aria, after which she and her former lover Marcello are reconciled.

LA BOHEME

The death-bed scene in Act IV. Rodolfo is distraught as Mimi coughs and breathes her last.

THE MAGIC FLUTE

Mozart's last opera provides wonderful opportunities for stagecraft, and has survived many peculiar versions. For the HOC, Jennifer Primrose has designed colourful, traditional sets, and Harvey Icepick has directed the comedy and its serious overtones with good humour.

In the first Act we meet all the main protagonists, including the high priest Sarastro, sung by a bass, the frolicsome bird-catcher Papageno who makes music with his pipe, and the three lads who will accompany the hero Tamino on his quest for the daughter of the Queen of Night.

The whole production is sparkling, with quick scene changes, the use of trap-doors and a pace which, even in the more solemn scenes, never flags.

THE MAGIC FLUTE

At the end of the 8th Scene in Act II, Papageno and Papagena engage in an enchanting and always popular duet, which is rattled off with delicacy and wit at great speed.

LUCIA DI LAMMERMOOR

Lucia is one of the great coloratura soprano roles, which was sung in the past by Patti, Melba and Tetrazzini, but also attracted the most important modern singers, Maria Callas and Joan Sutherland.

In terms of the HOC, it was only natural that Lucia should be reserved for Lina Carpaccia, whose voice can encompass the florid passage-work and whose acting ability makes the mad scene dramatically effective and something more than a vocal *tour de force*.

The HOC production soft-pedals the Scottish element of the story, for hamsters are not seen at their best in kilts.

TOSCA

Act II in the Farnese Palace. Scarpia, the tyrant 'before whom all Rome trembled', has had the singer Tosca brought to his apartments and tricked her into an arrangement which will presumably save the life of her lover Cavaradossi. But Tosca seeks to trick Scarpia too, and in this scene, having obtained his signature on a release, she stabs him with a fruit knife she has surreptitiously picked up from the table.

Those who have been privileged to watch the great Lina Carpaccia in this scene will never forget the passion she expresses with her rare voice and her body. The Scarpia of Herbert Jefferson is an excellent foil for her.

FAUST

Gounod's mid-nineteenth century opera concentrates on the love story of the scholar Faust and the beautiful Marguerite, and omits most of the other elements in the Goethe play from which it stems.

In the first scene, the aged philosopher Dr Faust bemoans the failure of his life and, in a moment of despair, calls on the Devil (Mephistopheles) to help him. Obliging as ever, Mephistopheles offers Faust his heart's desires, but demands the philosopher's soul in return. Faust hesitates at this price of fulfillment and happiness, but the wily Devil conjures up a vision of Marguerite at her spinning wheel, and Faust agrees at once.

Harvey Icepick directs a charming production of this opera, with Dora Llandu personifying the innocent heroine.

DER ROSENKAVALIER

In Act II of Richard Strauss's best-known opera, the young Count Octavian presents to Sophie von Faninal the silver rose which symbolizes the offer of marriage. Octavian comes as the representative of the boorish Baron Ochs von Lerchenau, but no one should be surprised that these two young people fall in love at first sight and are on their way to matrimony by the time the final curtain falls.

Gunther Winterstrebel brings a light Viennese touch to this toothsome soufflé of an opera (though he originates himself from Paderborn). The manly Octavian is a soprano role, and sung with great flair by Melanie Fiddler. Sophie, girlish but not shy, is successfully played by the pert Gudrun Spiess, who also sings Papagena in *The Magic Flute*.

FALSTAFF

Verdi's final opera, premiered in 1893, was based on Shakespeare's *The Merry Wives of Windsor*, and represented a fitting farewell to Verdi's long career.

In the HOC production, Falstaff is sung by the young baritone Felix Rathbone; here he is seen in Act II, singing Mistress Ford's praises while she plucks at her lute. He describes how handsome and slender he was as a boy, and prepares to make amorous advances – but is suddenly interrupted and becomes the butt of the merry wives' joke.

THE MARRIAGE OF FIGARO

Mozart's most popular opera is one of the HOC's mainstays. The critics had to pull out all their superlatives in reviewing its first performance. They uniformly praised its sets and costumes, its voices and the excellence of its direction.

Act I is full of bustling activity in the servants' quarters of Count Almaviva's castle near Seville as preparations are made for the barber's wedding. In this scene, the prospective bride Susanna, sung by Mercy Cristale, listens to the Count as he presses his unwelcome affections on her. Hiding in the armchair is the page Cherubino (sung by a soprano), who thinks he is in love with the Count's wife.

AIDA

Aida is surely the grandest of grand operas, and since its first performance in Cairo in 1871, all the great (and not so great) singers have attempted the title role.

The HOC production is majestic in concept, matching the grandeur of Verdi's music. The designer, Gian Eduardo Fuoco, has rightly gone for spectacle, and in this scene from Act II, in which the King of Egypt proclaims the triumph of Radames and his army, he has created a massive Temple of Ammon at the gates of Thebes. Radames loves the slave girl (really an Ethiopian princess), Aida; Aida returns this love; but the Egyptian princess Amneris also loves Radames. That is the crux of this straightforward tale of jealousy and betrayal, and it provides three robust and rewarding roles for Gino Peruzzi, Gabriella Concile and Clara La Jolla.

TRISTAN AND ISOLDE

Wagner's medieval love-drama was mounted by the HOC largely as a favour to Gunther Winterstrebel; neither Ugo Rondetto nor Filbert Broadstreet would have considered it essential to the repertoire. And yet Tilly Thunderbar and Rex Tremolo make a most appealing pair of lovers, and the production has found a surprisingly wide audience.

We see here the crucial scene in Act I when Isolde offers Tristan the love potion, thinking that it is a death potion. When he drinks from the goblet and does not die, they fall into each other's arms.

DON GIOVANNI

In Act II of Mozart's most brilliant opera, the Don and his servant Leporello, having cavorted through one adventure after another, meet unexpectedly in a gloomy churchyard. There they are startled to hear a voice from the grave of the Commendatore, whom Don Giovanni killed in a duel during Act I. Leporello quakes with fright, but Don Giovanni instructs him to invite the statue to supper that night.

The HOC statue of the Commendatore is a truly awesome creation and his appearance, bathed in a green light, at the supper scene strikes terror even into the irresponsible Don's heart.

TURANDOT

Puccini's vengeful and unyielding Chinese princess is another of Lina Carpaccia's great roles. In Act II, Scene II, she appears in imperial splendour to subject Prince Calaf to the three riddles, which no suitor has yet been able to solve. The bargain is death or marriage. Our hero, who has fallen in love with Turandot after one sight of her, solves the riddles with no hint of difficulty; but Turandot is still adamant about fulfilling her side of the bargain. In the last Act she is won over, her icy heart is melted by love, and everyone forgets about her former cruelty and disdain.

OTELLO

Ferruccio Nutti invests Verdi's Otello with unusual depth of character. He not only sings the magnificent music with controlled passion, but makes the Moor's suspicions and jealousy completely believable.

The bedroom scene in the last act is especially moving. First we have Desdemona's plaintive willow song, then her farewell to Emilia and her quiet *Ave Maria*.

Nutti makes Otello's entrance at this point a moment of frozen apprehension. Desdemona desperately denies all his accusations, but he strangles her nonetheless. Only moments later he learns that Desdemona was indeed innocent, and kills himself with a dagger.

A MIDSUMMER NIGHT'S DREAM

The opera of Benjamin Britten has been introduced into the HOC repertoire as a family entertainment. Young audiences react joyously to scenes like this one in Act II, when Tytania, affected by the magic juice Oberon has squeezed on her eyes, wakens and falls in love with the weaver Bottom, who has an ass's head.

The main conductor of the HOC orchestra, Crispin Pepperidge, is extremely adept at bringing out the magic of this gossamer score.